Every Color in My Mother Tongue

I0142544

Every Color in My
Mother Tongue

Ketevan Tsereteli

Published in the United States of America.
Book cover by Ketevan Tsereteli

Paperback ISBN: 979-8-9928459-1-4
Ebook ISBN: 979-8-9928459-0-7
Library of Congress Control Number: 2025904872

To my snow leopard

Growth

Blackberry

Grandma called me *Mayvala*,
blackberry in my mother tongue.
She was *Adga Bebo* to me,
the two fingers I held onto
when I was learning to walk.
Standing was difficult
for both of us back then.

Mchadi

Our bedroom walls
grew mossy fractals
in the winter.
We would huddle
around a camping stove
in the living room,
making corn bread
and telling stories
until we dozed off.

Walk and Multiply

Great-grandpa was a meteorologist
until Kazbegi ice
stole his leg in the 60s.
He taught Dad
to multiply.

Grandma was a civil engineer.
she called us *bachulebi*,
a word only she knew
the meaning of.
She showed me
how to walk.

Creases

I never liked folding
clothes. I couldn't
get the edges right. My
brother treated his
cotton like art. Precise
90° corners. He was
only three. I still wear
creases on my sleeves.

Cabbage

Mom would wrap my feet
in vinegar, my forehead
in crisp cabbage leaves
on those feverish days
I frequented
as a child.

Apple Juice

I peed my pants in class. I
hadn't learned the word
for hall pass. My best friend
tried to cover for me,
spilling apple juice
in her seat next to mine.

Front Row

On the first day of school,
I rushed to sit in front,
like Mom had.
A parent complained:
seeing me would interfere
with her son's education.
So I was moved to the back.
I hadn't learned to fend
for myself yet,
the girl whose mother
had flown abroad.

Kvevri

Great-grandma made wine
in tethered, tear-shaped vessels,
decanting hundreds of liters
by hand to preserve our tradition.
We never met, but I see her
sometimes in my strength.

Pansy Gardens

On our after school strolls
through pansy gardens,
I tried to synchronize
my step with yours
when you weren't looking.
It made me feel
part of something
bigger.

Conspicuous

When we moved,
my parents taught me
about lightning
from a cumulonimbus
and attention
from a gathering crowd.
I still feel uneasy
in flat terrain.

Premature

Grandpa was a veterinarian
at a chicken factory.
In time, the manager and
an endless supply of eggs.
But all we wanted was
more time with him.

Vanilla Pudding

Mom was phosphorescent
in those summer days
we visited her
in the chemistry department.
We read Harry Potter
in front of her office,
waiting for vanilla pudding
from the cafeteria.
I couldn't wait
to go to college.

All Nighter

Every few years
we moved.
Two suitcases,
a carry-on,
and a backpack each
to keep our days.
All nighters
at the gate,
one item strapped
to each limb.
We should have tied
them to our seats
instead.

Single Entry

Our stay
twice postponed
due to three months of silence.
Our arrival
bittersweet,
a decade without looking back.
Cutting ties
with our home
for a single entry stamp.

Adamiani

Grandpa was a painter, unshaken
in his respect for this world.
At times a builder or a boxer.
With a depth in the way he treated
others and a weightlessness when
he joked around with us kids.

Facing West

I grew up in rental
apartments pointing North
and didn't spend
time looking at sunsets.
Facing West
is like seeing the colors
of the universe
for the first time.

Memoir

Grandpa asked a favor only once, the day
before I left for college. "I have 10 pages of my
memoir. Can you help me finish it?"
He was the one who always helped others.

Promises had come easily back then. I lost his
handwritten notes at the first sign of struggle.
Even years later, I couldn't bear to tell him.

Now, I won't get the chance.

Race to Baku

We ratted overnight to Baku,
clinging to a 1970s rail wagon
and my last chance to reach
the embassy before it closed.
I was still shaking when I let go of
Dad to hand in the proof
of my existence.

Safety Pin

Grandma fends off
malevolent forces
with a three inch safety pin
on her blouse.
I use a blue pendant
and speak more of
my weakness
than my strength.

Distress

Ablaze

My organs are on fire.
  Inadequate efferent signals.
I set my whole body ablaze.
Burn off my fingertips.
Rewire my network.
Relearn how to breathe.

Nine Months

Nine months for a name
I wrestle from strangers
to validate my symptoms.
I didn't learn to complain
enough, only to endure.
Was it always painful to be living?

Offering

These days
I feel my mortality
close by.
A murmur has begun
in my lower left ribs.
I shall bring an offering,
give up the city I call home,
to undo what last April
set in motion.

Second Lifetime

I'm on my second lifetime.
Last century, I wouldn't have
made it past forty.
I guess I'm lucky then
to be born in my time,
with access to healthcare.

Dear Nurse

Do you remember me?
I'm the one without veins.
The one you prick and search
to find a source.
The one whose arm turns to ice
when the flow is reversed.
The one who counts to ten
and imagines his smile
on the other side.

Marzipan

My winter is bitter marzipan
in concentric circles
pulled apart
by eager fingers
in ritual fever
for the new.

Fracture

There's a weight
suspended from
my rib cage. I
write letters to
the ones I hold
dear, to get out
what is unsaid
before I fracture. I
can't talk
face-to-face. Each
conversation sends me
spiraling.

Distortion

Teal with gold
specks in his eyes,
his picture
out of focus.
A shrill glare.
My eyebrow throbs,
splits me in two.
Have I done
something wrong?
Why am I like this
again?

Depths

I cling to my pen
as I spiral.
Easier than holding
on to your back.
Don't want to drag you
into these depths.

Time Travel

I can't focus.
The glare of this world
is too much when
someone is drilling
into my left temple.
I keep slipping
back to a year ago.

Santorini

I'm anxious of meeting
more milestones alone.
I'm holding onto our
four years so tightly,
I get tendinitis.
Still learning to drift
with you instead of
apart, until we
make it to Santorini.

Durable

In constant maintenance
of organs rooted
in our bow
      polishing
      aligning
      adjusting.
Why not pull out
all of our teeth
and replace them
with something more
durable?

Chaotic

I hold my breath
as the streets exhale
periodically.
A soporific veil
washing over
unsuspecting passersby,
sprawling, stretching,
in chaotic motion.

Ascidian

Among iridescent ceruleans and violets
  and a flood of perfumes,
I found this ridge
   that I call my new home.
I'll keep filtering my water
and stay for good,
   as I digest my own brain
in this metropolis.

Jellyfish

It's worse at night
in my shallow bed.
I'm careful, but
these tiny jellyfish
sting, relentless
in   my
ovary,   arch,
  palm,   rib.
I ask   him
to check   on me
    in thirty   minutes
  in case   I'm not
breath   -ing.

Repair

Swedish Massage

The act of writing
is a Swedish massage
for the brain:
A gentle pressure
that loosens the knots
I developed
from staring at my screen
too much.

Long Words

Synchronous interactions are draining,
Their response time and format.
Sometimes I have trouble speaking.
Compression helps.
It's poetry.
As Rustaveli said, *long words spoken shortly.*[1]

---

[1]S. Rustaveli, *The Knight in the Panther's Skin*, trans. L. Coffin, Tbilisi, POEZIA Press, 2015, p. 12

Every Day

It's no longer about
expressing my individuality
or my preferences.
It's about survival. So I
      eat the same dish,
      sleep the same way,
      take the same walk,
at the same time
      every day
      for the rest of my life
if I have to.

How to Digest Food

The same four meals a day,
twelve ounces each.
Dad makes nostalgic jokes
as he washes the vegetables.
"Plan for children
while I can still help,"
he says.
I count to twenty
with each bite.

Fog

My thought starts
as a sphere in my head,
one I can't quite grasp.
I reduce it to a line
projected onto this canvas.
If I create a superposition
of every page I've written,
will I be able to hold
a conversation again?

That Part of Me

I started getting migraines
    after ten minutes
    of a board game.
I started working again
    because I didn't want
    that part of me
    to die.
The part of me that
    solves problems
    and thinks strategically.
The part of me that
    held my dreams
    and I was finally proud of.

Solar Winds

When my tulips start to slouch,
I'll leave them on life support
and make my way across 66.5°N,
chasing charged particles from
the sun colliding
with our atmosphere.

I Would Not Be a Computer Scientist

In those days
computers used to be busy all day.
You could pay for some time,
if you knew who to talk to.
But you would need to bring your own tape
and punch cards.
I would not be a computer scientist
in those days.

Sever

I'm in a precarious
headspace today.
Best avoid confrontation,
lest I sever ties
I was never meant
to break.

Solar Panels

I'm thinking of installing
solar panels
on my shoulders.
When I meet people
outdoors, I'll recharge
as long as the weather holds.

This Is Enough

I don't need a house
or an electric car.
This is enough.

Children don't need
much space.
I grew up sharing a bedroom
with my brother.

I am enough.
I want to stop
trying so hard
now.

Hydrated

I'm waiting
for the rest of my life.
In the meantime,
I'm staying hydrated.

Laughing Too Hard

I long for Wednesday dinners
with my family.
Mom's *khachapuri*,
   second only to Grandma's,
Dad's vision for
   the future of science,
Or my tears from
   laughing too hard
   at my brother's banter.
The cost of being ambitious
and an immigrant.

Physical Therapy

I was happy today, lying in grass as the clouds
slid by and I lifted the sky for exercise.
A change in perspective from
waiting for the rest of my life
or for the day I wake up
feeling better.

Dinners and Drives

Time with Dad.
Growing up, conversations on drives.
Now, over dinners for my rehabilitation.
Easier as adults, learning from difference.
I'm lucky for this time.
He didn't have it with his.

Sideways

I'm relaxing,
head on the table,
seeing the world
sideways.
Seagulls drifting vertically.
Everyone looking up
for a change.

Sun-Dried Clothes

I want to smell the sun
on my pillowcase and
taste the strawberries
on the balcony.
I want a simpler life
with bees so delicate to petals
and fresh baked buns on Sundays when
everything else is closed.

This Year

I always carry snacks in my pockets:
　　chocolates on the left,
　　crackers on the right.
When I meet a friend in the street, we exchange
sweets instead of pleasantries.

Captivating

It comes so naturally to you,
tuning your life to this new me.
You slow your pace,
read me Lovecraft,
place your hand in mine
when nothing else helps the aches.

Daydream

Whale Galaxy

NASA was busy
taking a panorama of
the Whale Galaxy
the day we met.
It's the size of
our Milky Way,
30M light years away.
We could settle
there instead.

Caramel Frappuccino

We spoke of Kant
and Descartes
until the caramel
frappuccino melted
in your fingers
and the others left
to tour the Globe.
I hadn't felt understood
until you
and our time in London.

Endless

You are the feeling of home
in a place I haven't lived.
The dusk that stretches to dawn
as we ponder the universe.
You lay your head on my lap.
I stroke your hair.

Egg Yolk

You carried me on your back
after I sprained my ankle
at the amusement park.
On the bus ride home,
we received a remedy from a stranger:
egg yolk smeared on the skin and left overnight.

Movie Hop

Back then,
you couldn't reserve
seats at the movies.
So we would wait
in line, an hour,
sometimes two,
and sneak into
a second one.
We were students then,
and time was generous.

Kintsugi

We could have
been twins
in your childhood
photos. But I
didn't know
boundaries
when we first met.
I almost broke
us then. Now I like
seeing the gold
in our fractures.

Gentle with Yourself

Resilience
is your bright eyes
on your worst days
as you still pick up the phone
or that August 1st
you saved
someone's life
or the times you are gentle
with yourself
and with me.

I Wrote Her

I like
who I was
twelve years ago.
Optimistic,
outward looking.
I wrote her
a play,
to treasure her
when my mind
fades.

Vani

Your summer nights were foot baths with your
cousins. Feet propped on the edge of the
bucket, waiting for the water to cool. The
sound of the adults playing backgammon and
every once in a while
a thud
as a pear fell
and started tumbling
down the hill in the garden.

Snow Leopard

We celebrate five years
with two chairs from dear friends and family
who landed last night:
the owl and the goldfish.
You're the snow leopard,
and I'm the wolf.

Bermuda

You remind me of the ocean
and the conch shell you carried
from Bermuda. Like the rest of us,
a few chips and cracks over the years,
but an all the more beautiful
fragment of living.

Days Like These

Days like these don't come by often.
Little good mornings,
impromptu photo shoots,
late-night reflections with wine.
I'm glad I get them with you.
The other side of the world
doesn't feel so far
when it has you in it.

Larkspur

Your larkspur lived
for three weeks.
I'll press the petals
and bind them
into rectangles
to mark your books
since you like to read.

Golf Cart

That frigid winter,
you drove me to class
in a golf cart
every day.
Your knuckles would freeze.
but you were so cheerful,
I forgot my broken ankle.
you are the kind of friend
I hope to be.

Snow in July

You are the snow in July
on the peaks of my homeland.
A welcome reprieve from
the sweltering summer
and the cacophony of the city.
A fragment of ease and artistry.

Sail with Dolphins

I hope you flourish,
    live at ease,
        make music,
      receive the care of
              others.
    Above all, I hope you sail
often with dolphins.

Gratitude

You are the path that changes
someone's life, the older brother with
a motorcycle who is steadfast in times of
struggle. When you go the extra mile for
someone,
I hope they follow.

Dreaming

Seeing you again
is reviving
a part of myself
I forgot
I needed.
The part that plays games
and laughs
and spends time
dreaming.

Turmeric

Your love is the playful exchange
of garlands at sunset,
the marigold petals dipped in
turmeric at your feet,
the soft gaze that meets yours
when you start to waver.

We Are Not of This Solar System

Our solar system is still young.
Iron and other elements are yet to be formed.
I'm space dust from Andromeda.
Which galaxy are you from?

Olympus Mons

A blue sunset
frames the skyline
at the base of Olympus Mons.
Everything is provided for,
   travel, room and board,
as long as we agree
to never come back.

Hemocyanin

If we needed copper
instead of iron
to transport O_2,
we would bleed blue,
become vegetarian,
and stick to our predators.

Salmon Sunsets

Your heartbeat the cobalt,
salmon of sunsets
in Nordic harbors.
The moon reflected
in your lashes
as you lull me to sleep.
A drowsy kiss
on my nose.
You are everything,
every color in my mother tongue.

About the Author

Ketevan Tsereteli is a computer scientist, illustrator, and poet. Her writing explores themes of heritage and personal growth. She holds a B.A. from Princeton University.